Multiplication Football

Book Five of
The Gift of Numbers
Math Fantasy Curriculum

Rachel Rogers and Joe Lineberry

Illustrations by ARTE RAVE

an imprint of
PROSPECTIVE PRESS LLC
1959 Peace Haven Rd, #246, Winston-Salem, NC 27106 U.S.A.
www.prospectivepress.com

Published in the United States of America by PROSPECTIVE PRESS LLC

MULTIPLICATION FOOTBALL

Text copyright © Rachel Rogers and Joe Lineberry, 2021
All rights reserved.
The authors' moral rights have been asserted.

Illustrations by ARTE RAVE
© Prospective Press, 2021
All rights reserved.
The illustrator's moral rights have been asserted.

ISBN 978-1-943419-10-4

ProP-G002

Multiplication Football is the fifth volume in the Gift of Numbers math fantasy curriculum. For information on additional volumes in the series or for bulk sales, please send inquiries to education@prospectivepress.com

Printed in the United States of America
First paperback printing March, 2021

The text of this book is typeset in Mouse Memoirs
Accent text is typeset in Galindo

PUBLISHER'S NOTE

This book is a work of creative non-fiction with fictional fantasy elements. The people, names, characters, locations, activities, and events portrayed or implied by this book are the product of the author's imagination or are used fictitiously. Any resemblance to actual people, locations, and events is strictly coincidental. No actual numbers disappeared during the writing of this book.

Without limiting the rights as reserved in the above copyright, no part of this publication may be reproduced, stored in or introduced into any retrieval system, or transmitted—by any means, in any form, electronic, mechanical, photocopying, recording, or otherwise—without the prior written permission of the publisher. Not only is such reproduction illegal and punishable by law, but it also hurts the authors and illustrator who toiled hard on the creation of this work and the publisher who brought it to the world. In the spirit of fair play, and to honor the labor and creativity of the authors and illustrator, we ask that you purchase only authorized electronic and print editions of this work and refrain from participating in or encouraging piracy or electronic piracy of copyright-protected materials. Please give creators a break and don't steal this or any other work.

Dedicated to our incredible in-laws:

A Review of the Plot of our Story

Our odd and even number friends have had lots of fun in our first four books. Let's review what has happened to them so far. This will help you get ready for their adventures in *Multiplication Football*.

Saved by Addition—The odd and even numbers did not like each other. They were different. King More dreamed future boys and girls would need more numbers. Doctor Even created addition. It was the first math operation. The even and odd numbers enjoyed working together with addition to make new numbers.

Surprised by Subtraction—King Less realized future girls and boys would need to find the difference between two numbers. Doctor Odd and Doctor Even created a new math operation. It was called subtraction. The doctors were surprised when they subtracted a number from itself (like 6 – 6). Ghostly Zero was born. Almost immediately, numbers started to disappear. The odd and even numbers were glad to live in fact families. Using fact families, they could always bring back a missing number.

Graphing the Mystery—King More and King Less wanted help solving the mystery of the missing numbers. Detective Science helped them find data on when the numbers disappeared. Graph Giraffe explained how to put the data in easy-to-read graphs. The graphs showed that Ghostly Zero might be causing the numbers to disappear. The graphs also showed that numbers disappeared more often in the afternoon. Ghostly Zero might not be the cause. Detective Science agreed to work on a way to use data to solve this mystery.

Adventure with Fractions—Breaking news! Number 3 became the first number to disappear and then come back without using his fact family. King Less was impatient. He did not want to wait on Detective Science. He wanted to solve the mystery a different way. He and some friends went to the mountains to find Dream Princess. They hoped she had a magic formula that would keep numbers from disappearing. Dream Princess said one of her popular formulas helped numbers disappear. Of course, King Less did not want that formula. She then used fractions to make a formula that might keep numbers from disappearing.

A buzz of excitement filled Odd Nation and Even Land. The numbers couldn't stop talking about King Less's visit with Dream Princess.

"I heard King Less got a magic formula to stop our numbers from disappearing. Detective Science is studying the magic formula."

"Number 3 said the princess's friends want to disappear."

"Dream Princess is a ghostly zero."

"I heard the princess vanished while King Less was talking to her."

"It was on the news. Even and odd numbers play football together."

Now that was big news! The odd and even numbers had learned that working and living together made their lives better. But they had never played together.

While visiting the princess, King Less heard that odd and even numbers played football with each other there. King More and King Less decided to try it too.

They planned a big football game. Even numbers on one team would play against odd numbers on the other team. The kings were delighted. The even number team could now score 3-point field goals and 1-point extra points. The odd number football team could now score 6-point touchdowns and 2-point safeties.

What a great game this would be!

The even and odd numbers selected their football coaches for the big game. **Coach 9 Winner** would coach the odd number team. **Coach 4 Success** would coach the even number team.

Football teams need a lot of big players. So each coach ran to his doctor and asked him to make more big numbers.

Doctor Even listened to Coach Success's request. He started by adding 8 to itself nine times. 8 + 8 + 8 + 8 + 8 + 8 + 8 + 8 + 8 = 72. He had to repeat the addition nine times, so it took all day in Operation Room A to make one big 72 football player.

8 + 8 = 16
16 + 8 = 24
24 + 8 = 32
32 + 8 = 40
40 + 8 = 48
48 + 8 = 56
56 + 8 = 64
64 + 8 = 72

Coach Winner insisted that Doctor Odd do the same thing. He used repeated addition with 9s to create a big odd number. He added 9 to itself eight times. 9 + 9 + 9 + 9 + 9 + 9 + 9 + 9 = 72. Doctor Odd's addition operations took the entire day, too.

9 + 9 = 18
18 + 9 = 27
27 + 9 = 36
36 + 9 = 45
45 + 9 = 54
54 + 9 = 63
63 + 9 = 72

Late that afternoon, Doctor Even and Doctor Odd met with each other. "Wow! Did you see that?" asked Doctor Even. "Adding nine 8s equals 72, and adding eight 9s equals 72. The sums are the same. I wonder if there is a faster math operation that could do these calculations? It could replace repeated addition."

The two doctors were excited. They went to their lab to discover a new math operation. Around noon the next day, the two doctors were standing in their lab with Coach Success and Coach Winner. As you might expect, they did discover a new math operation, called "multiplication." They were explaining it to the two coaches.

"Multiplication is fast," explained Doctor Odd. "Instead of adding 8 to itself nine times, you just multiply 8 x 9 = 72. Look, it works the other way too—9 x 8 = 72. We can get bigger numbers quickly when we use multiplication."

"It makes sense that they both equal 72," said Doctor Even. "Look at these two arrays. The one on top is 9 rows of 8 blocks. The one on the bottom is 8 rows of 9 squares. Each array has the same number of squares—72. That proves 8 x 9 = 9 x 8, and they both equal 72."

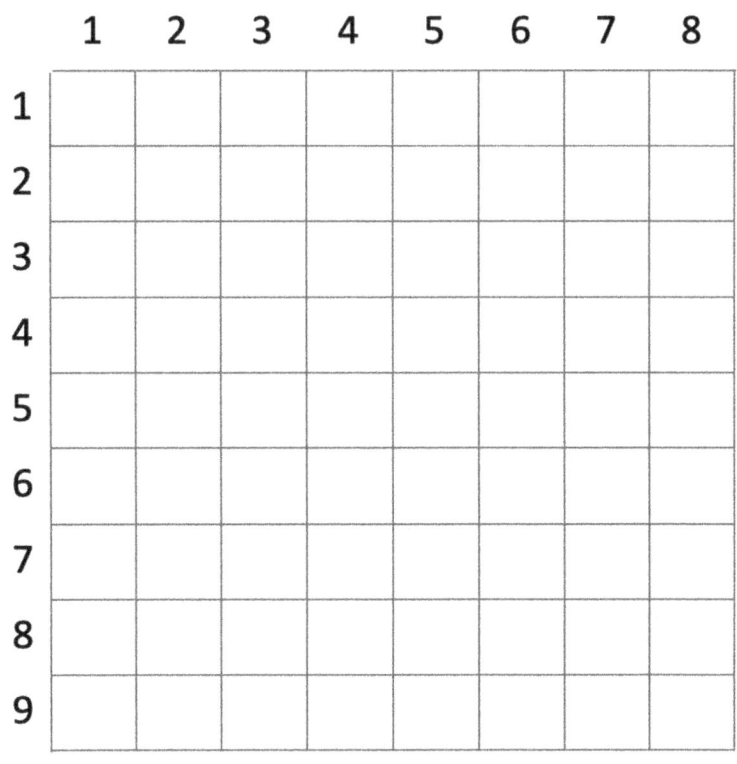 = 72 squares!

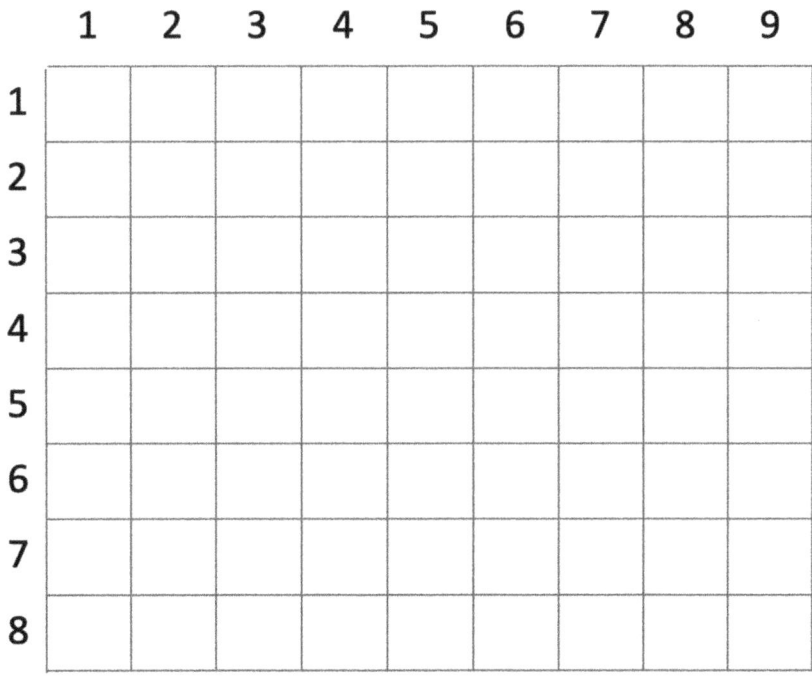 = 72 squares!

"But this doesn't make sense," exclaimed Coach Winner. "Doctor Odd, you created a big number, but it is an even number 72. You made another big number for the even number team."

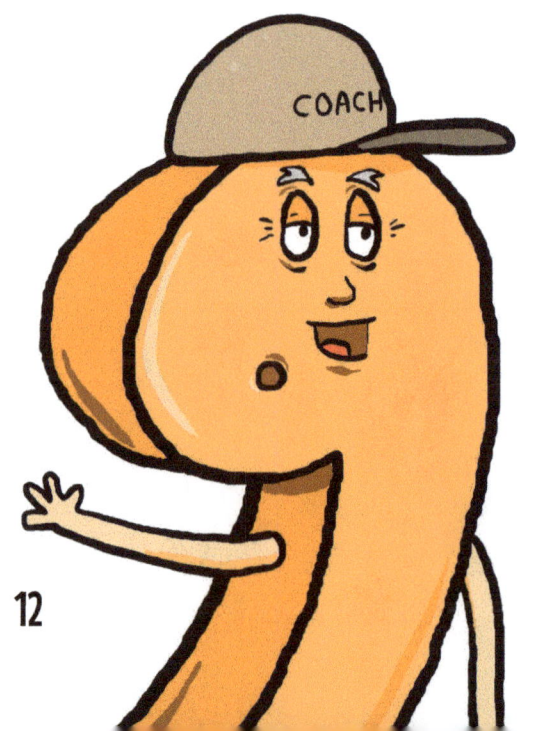

Doctor Odd was embarrassed. Then he started laughing at himself. "I was working so hard on this project. I overlooked this point," he said. "I am supposed to make big odd numbers. Thanks, Coach. We should always step back and see if our math solutions make sense."

"No worries," continued Doctor Odd. "We can get an odd number. We learned a pattern when we invented the addition operation. This pattern is pretty obvious when you look at the repeated addition we did yesterday."

"Adding two odd numbers (like 63 and 9) makes an even number (like 72). But adding an even and odd number (like 54 and 9) makes an odd number (like 63). All I need to do is add any odd number to 72 to make the sum an odd number. Let's add 9."

"Multiplication is the newest member of the Operation Club," said Doctor Odd. "Remember this: Like 'sum' is the answer to an addition operation, 'product' is the answer to a multiplication operation."

Doctor Even leaned over to Coach Success. He whispered, "You know, we could make an even bigger number. Let's multiply 72 x 10. That would equal a big 720."

Coach Success looked disappointed. "Good idea," said the coach. "But it won't work. Our football helmets are only big enough for two-digit numbers."

"Okay," replied the doctor. "So what is the largest two-digit even number we can make?"

Doctor Odd overheard their conversation. "I know," he interrupted. "It must be less than 100. Your biggest even two-digit number will be 98. Our largest odd number will be a little bigger—99."

1	2	3	4	5	6	7	8	9	10
11	12	13	14	15	16	17	18	19	20
21	22	23	24	25	26	27	28	29	30
31	32	33	34	35	36	37	38	39	40
41	42	43	44	45	46	47	48	49	50
51	52	53	54	55	56	57	58	59	60
61	62	63	64	65	66	67	68	69	70
71	72	73	74	75	76	77	78	79	80
81	82	83	84	85	86	87	88	89	90
91	92	93	94	95	96	97	98	99	100

"So how can we use multiplication to make these numbers quickly?" asked Coach Winner.

"Let's use 10. It's always easy to multiply by 10," said Doctor Odd. "We know 10 x 10 = 100, which is the smallest three-digit number. Then subtract 2 to equal 98, or subtract 1 to equal 99."

Over the next few days, they learned some new math facts about multiplication.

"Here's a cool fact," said Doctor Odd. "We know multiplying any number by 10 is easy—like 4 x 10. That's equal to 4 tens. So you just move the four to the tens place and then put a 0 in the ones place. It equals 40."

"You can then work other problems with 10. What is 4 x 9? Well, 9 is 1 less than 10. So:

Multiply	4 x 10 = 40
Subtract 4 one time	−4
Your answer is	36

So 4 x 9 = 36."

$$40 = \underbrace{\text{🏈🏈}}_{20} + \underbrace{\text{🏈🏈}}_{20}$$

"Or what about multiplying by 5? What is 4 x 5? Since 5 is half of 10:

4 x 5 = half of 40.

If you divide 40 into two equal parts, each part is 20. So 4 x 5 = 20."

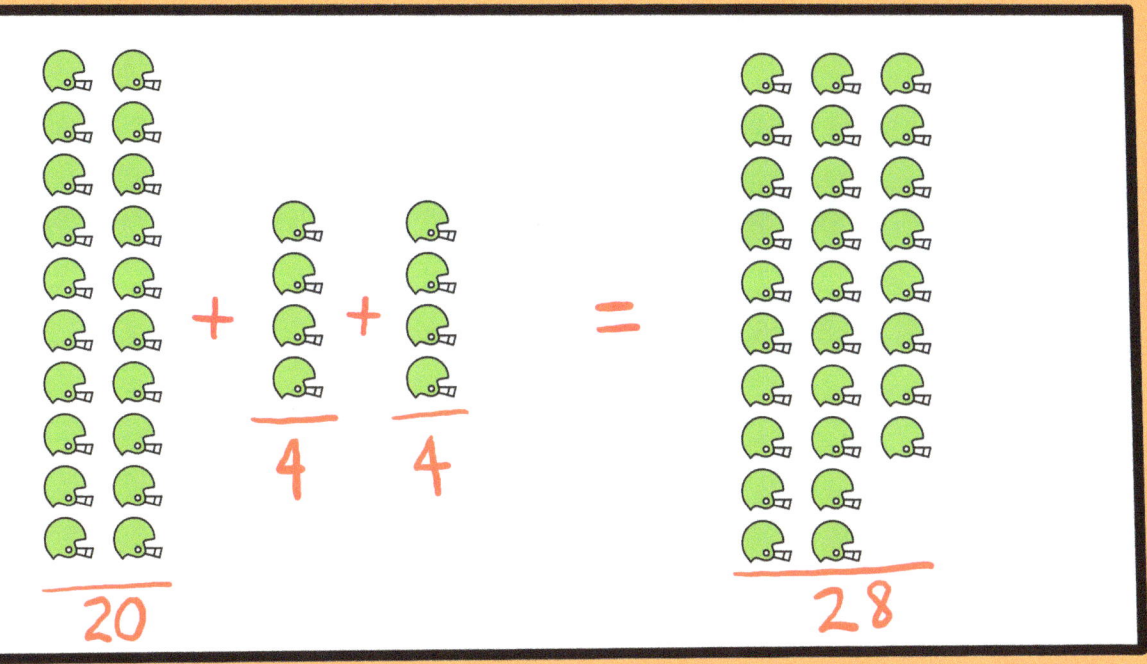

"Then try multiplying by 7. What is 4 x 7? Since 7 is 2 more than 5:

Multiply	4 x 5 = 20
Add 4 two times	+ 4
	+ 4
Your answer is	28

Here are two more easy facts:

Any number times 0 = 0, so 4 x 0 = 0

Any number times 1 = that number, so 4 x 1 = 4."

The day of the football game finally arrived. The football stadium was full of fans from Odd Nation and Even Land. It was a hot, sunny day, so the coaches were glad that the local grocery store had donated all their bottles of mountain water to the teams to drink.

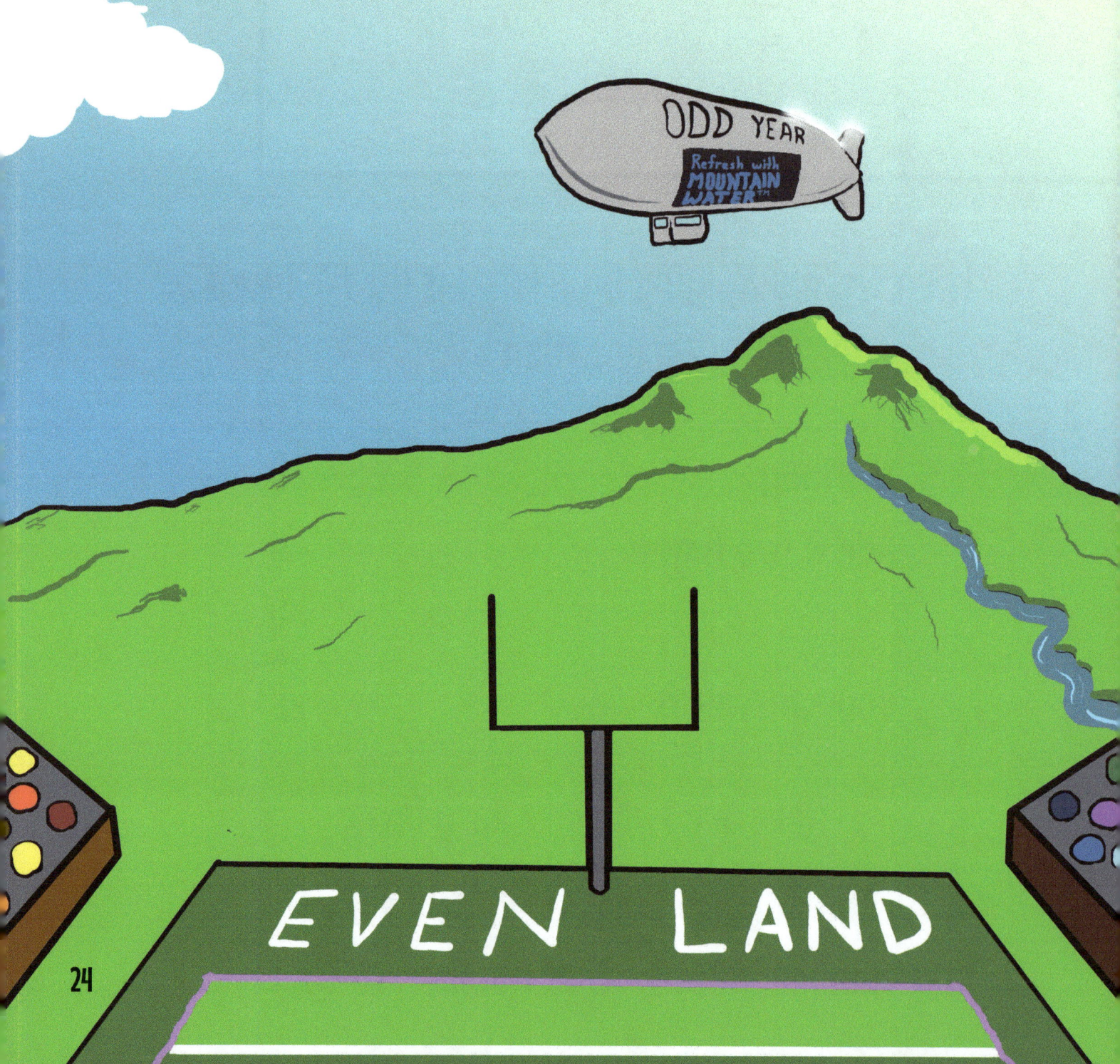

King Less had also given the odd team another drink. He had secretly supplied the odd football team with the magic formula drink from Dream Princess. You remember, the one that was designed to keep numbers from disappearing.

He wanted to make sure his odd football team stayed on the field for the whole game.

The kings and Detective Science were in their seats talking to each other, while the football teams were warming up on the field. King Less did not tell them about giving the magic formula to his team. Instead, he told them about work he had done on the football field.

"Look at the purple ribbon stapled in the ground around the field," said King Less. "I wanted to have bright ribbon to mark the perimeter of the field."

"We had to figure out how much ribbon to buy, so we used this equation to calculate the perimeter of our rectangular field. Length + Length + Width + Width = Perimeter."

"The football field is 100 yards long and 53 yards wide. So 100 + 100 + 53 + 53 = 306 yards. We bought 306 yards of purple ribbon."

King More added, "That is cool. You know, you could have used multiplication to make this easier. You could have used this equation:

$$100 \times 2 = 200 \text{ yards}$$
$$53 \times 2 = \underline{+106} \text{ yards}$$
$$306 \text{ yards of purple ribbon}"$$

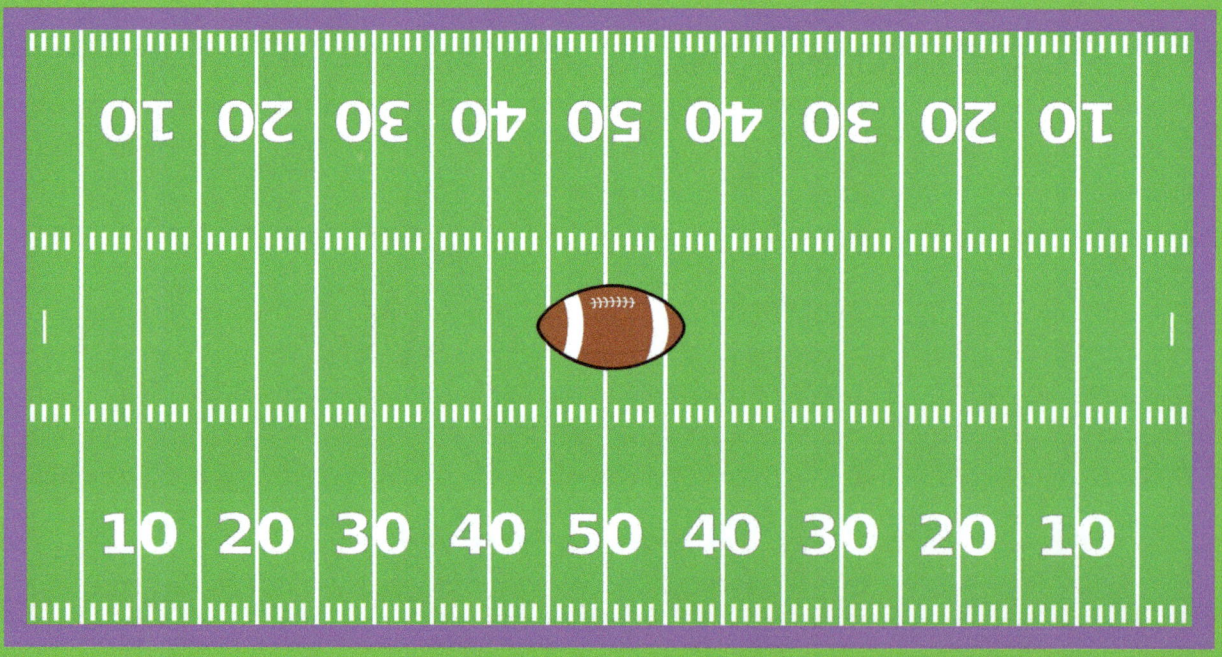

King Less was not listening. Instead, he was staring at the football field. Two even number football players had disappeared during their warmups. Lineman number 76 was gone, and punter number 32 vanished. The football he had been holding was now bouncing around on the ground.

At first King Less was feeling proud that only even number players were gone, but then three odd number players vanished. He screamed, "Noooooo! This can't be happening to my team. Why isn't my magic formula working?"

The fans and the football players were scared. More football players were vanishing, and no one knew what to do. All the numbers were scrambling to get out of the football stadium. All, except Detective Science. He was down on the field, looking for clues.

King More grabbed a microphone and tried to calm the crowd, "There is no need to panic. You know what to do. Find your fact families. Use our math operations to bring the missing numbers back."

"Future girls and boys need our numbers. We WILL stop our numbers from disappearing!"

To help the odd and even numbers bring back large numbers quickly, King More and King Less created multiplication fact families. Use the three numbers on the roof to fill in the blanks inside each house, making four different equations with these fact families.

The Publisher hereby grants permission to the original purchaser and/or sole owner of this book to make copies of this page for in-class use only. Copies may not be transmitted, sold, lent, or stored—electronically or otherwise.

Multiplication Football Exercise

Measure the length of the front cover of *Multiplication Football*. Round to the nearest inch.

Length = _____

Measure the width of the front cover of *Multiplication Football*. Round to the nearest inch.

Width = _____

Using these measurements, calculate the perimeter of the front cover of *Multiplication Football*.

1. Use addition to calculate the perimeter. Show your work.

Perimeter = _____

2. Use multiplication to calculate the perimeter. Show your work.

Perimeter = _____

Using these measurements, calculate the area of the front cover of *Multiplication Football*. (Hint: Area = Length X Width). Show your work.

Area = _____

Discussion Questions

1. Where did the two kings get the idea of playing a football game between the even and odd numbers?

2. On page 2, the numbers are sharing rumors about what happened when King Less went to see Dream Princess. Based on what you remember from *Adventure with Fractions*, which one of the four rumors on page 2 did not really happen?

3. Why did King Less calculate the perimeter of the football field?

4. Explain why multiplication is better than repeated addition.

5. Give some examples of multiplication facts in the story. Tell the strategy you use to find the product in each example.

6. Why do you think the authors wrote *Multiplication Football?*

The Publisher hereby grants permission to the original purchaser and/or sole owner of this book to make copies of this page for in-class use only. Copies may not be transmitted, sold, lent, or stored—electronically or otherwise.

Fact Family Exercise Solutions

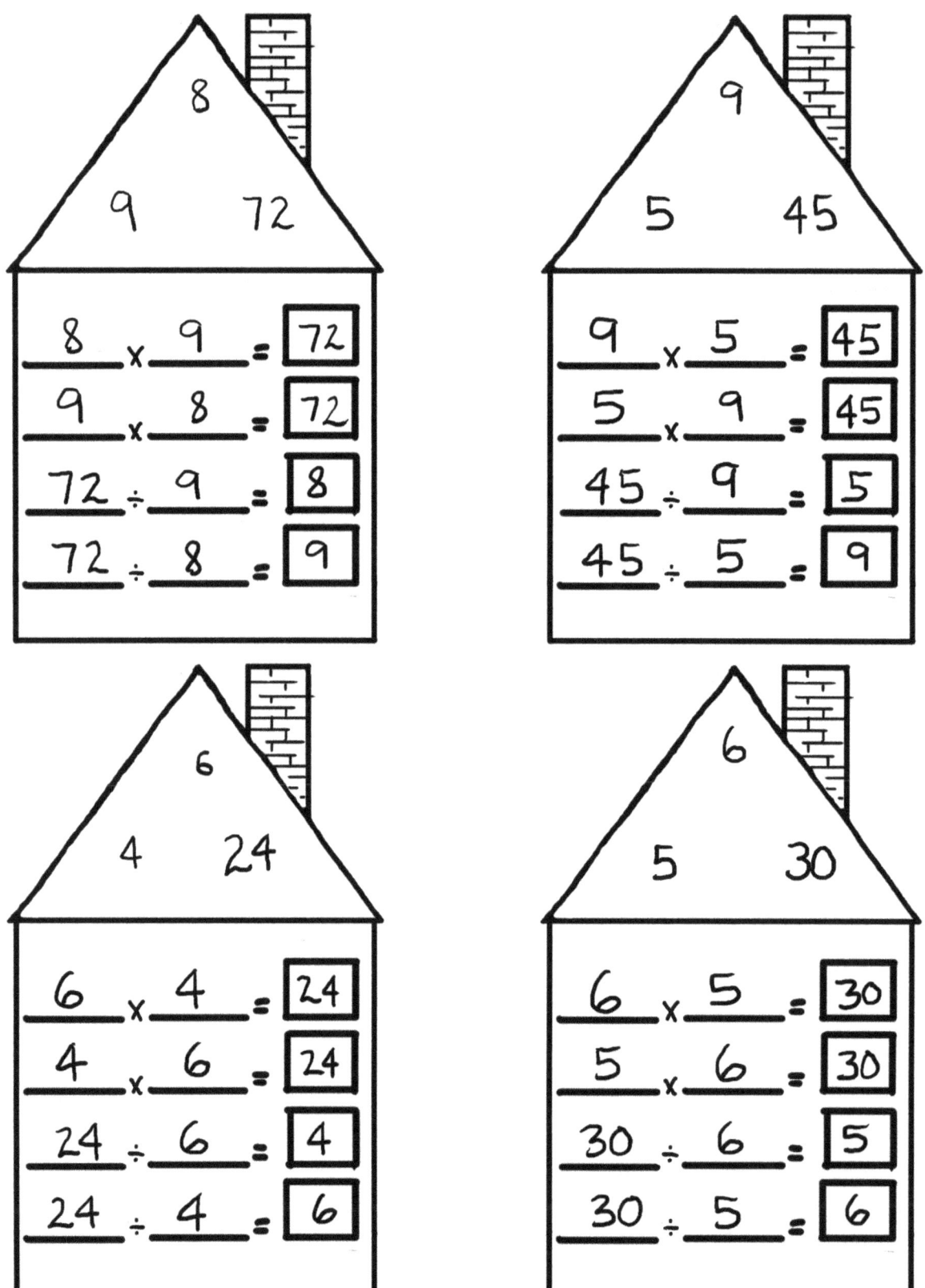

The Publisher hereby grants permission to the original purchaser and/or sole owner of this book to make copies of this page for in-class use only. Copies may not be transmitted, sold, lent, or stored—electronically or otherwise.

About the Authors

Rachel Rogers
retired from Old Richmond Elementary School, Winston-Salem, NC, after more than 42 years of teaching first, second, and third graders.

Joe Lineberry
told similar stories to his sons when they were growing up. He is also the author of *Let's Stop Playing Games: Finding Freedom in Authentic Living.*

About the Books

The Gift of Numbers
is a math fantasy curriculum that combines literature and mathmatics in a fun, age-appropriate series for second- and third-grade students.

- Volume 1: *Saved by Addition*
- Volume 2: *Surprised by Subtraction*
- Volume 3: *Graphing the Mystery*
- Volume 4: *Adventure with Fractions*
- Volume 5: *Multiplication Football*
- Volume 6: *The Experiment Game*
- Volume 7: *Division Gymnastics*

www.ingramcontent.com/pod-product-compliance
Lightning Source LLC
Chambersburg PA
CBHW051355110526
44592CB00024B/2989